BARSTOW

DEPOTS AND HARVEY HOUSES

By GERMAINE L. RAMOUNACHOU MOON

1978 view of the western veranda facing Barstow depot
(David Ottalini photo — Barstow Harvey House Society collection)

A Mojave River Valley Museum Association Publication
P.O. Box 1282
Barstow, California, 1980

BARSTOW Depots and Harvey Houses

Library of Congress Catalog Card No. 80-80936

ISBN No. 0-918614-02-3

Printed in the United States of America of an un-published copyrighted manuscript by Germaine L. Ramounachou-Moon with her permission.

Printing by Franklin Press

FOREWORD

Most people question only the history of the present Barstow Amtrak depot because it is still here. They ask why such a magnificent structure stands forlornly along the Atchison, Topeka & Santa Fe Railway's tracks . . . Few persons remember Fred Harvey's passenger accommodations and naught is left to reminisce or remind us of the bygone era when railroads were the indispensable link between two oceans, and the life-line of the desert communities.

If we let the Casa del Desierto join the rubbles of the past, future generations will lose parts of their rightful heritage and the essence of Barstow itself; a town created and sustained partly by and because of the railroad's development. To preserve and perpetuate visual evidences of such heritage, we must take responsible action before it is too late and perform our public duty.

This essay was prepared to fulfill some of these duties. It is a contribution to the needs of the concerned parties who have worked so faithfully saving tangible examples of the past. For some, these were photographs, bits of memorabilia, historical accounts, or an old building. In most cases, it was simply a fundamental desire to help a cause or other people quench a thirst for knowledge.

In assembling some of the pertinent data on the past and present Barstow passenger facilities, this researcher received the assistance of others for which she is immensely grateful, but couldn't possibly list all of them individually for fear of forgetting someone. Thank you to all my help-mates whether you proofread my terrible prose, made suggestions, spurred me to work, typed the manuscript, or patiently stood by. Thank you for being a friend.

Not being a writer, but merely a curious student of long forgotten details regarding the perpetual changes that occurred in the Mojave Desert and for reasons behind each development, this author is appreciative of the Mojave River Valley Museum Association members for publishing her efforts. We hope the readers will find this pamphlet useful.

In collecting and choosing the photographs, and for reproducing the selection, we are beholden to Annice Gibson for her help, and Fred Gibson for his lab work.

Barstow, 1980   Germaine L. Ramounachou Moon

This January, 1886 view of Barstow, taken from B Hill, shows the California Southern Railroad's first passenger facilities under construction at their location east from the route junction with the Atlantic & Pacific main line. The two story depot-hotel, supposedly a brick building, burned on July 8, 1887. It was immediately replaced by wooden, separate structures. Note the railroad box car sitting near the tracks, the temporary platform made of ties, and the passengers boarding the eastbound train. The residential section north of the tracks became known as the Lilienthal Subdivision. Very few details about this first land development at Barstow have survived in the San Bernardino County archives. *(San Bernardino County Museum — Belden Collection)*

BARSTOW DEPOTS AND HARVEY HOUSES

The story of the magnificent Casa del Desierto, Barstow's fourth depot-hotel began long before it was actually built. In fact, its roots were planted by the railroad companies that pioneered passenger accommodations in the Mojave Desert. Its fame is the story of Fred Harvey, a restaurateur par excellence and the hostelry proctor for the Atchison, Topeka & Santa Fe Railway Company. Once it was the heart of Barstow, a town created and sustained partly by and because of Santa Fe local developments.

On July 27, 1866, an Act of Congress mandated the Southern Pacific Railroad to construct a rail line south from San Francisco, then eastward to a point near The Needles, on the Colorado River. Here SP was to join the rails of the Atlantic & Pacific Railroad. The latter was chartered by the same Act of Congress to build westward from Springfield, Missouri, to The Needles.

Withstanding the 1973 financial panic and an enormous growth, SP began their Colorado Division branch line from Mojave, Kern County, in February, 1882. In mid October, they bridged the Mojave River southeast from the Waterman & Porter Quartz Mill establishing a freight station named Waterman on the south bank of the river. We do not know if SP erected buildings at the site which is now an area between the Riverside Drive railroad crossing and the northeast corner of Barstow Santa Fe diesel shop grounds. On old photographs, the site would be at the eastern part of the bend made by the original tracks, almost a mile from the old Harvey House.

The October 21, 1882, Calico Print, a local newspaper, reported on a week old celebration which had been held at the new Waterman station. Here fifteen couples, including Calicoans, attended a ball, enjoyed excellent music, a fine "collation" and a dance called "mazy". The paper further stated "that regular passenger cars and U.S. mail services will run to Waterman on and after the 23rd instant". However, SP selected Calico Junction, 10 miles east, for their eating place, depot, telegraph office, etc. . . Called Calico Station, the town was rechristened Daggett when Walter James, a local merchant, submitted the name to the Post Office Department on February 26, 1883.

It is unlikely that SP built the Daggett Railroad Eating House which, over the years, became the Stone Hotel, now a registered landmark under the care of the San Bernardino County Museum. That business appeared to have been an entirely private enterprise independent from railroad affairs, except for the land on which it stood. In fact the land, including Daggett townsite and the whole of Section 21, belonged to the South-

RAILROAD HOTEL.

V. VAN BRIESEN, Proprietor,

DAGGETT STATION,

San Bernardino Co., Cal.

The Eating Station for all Passenger Trains of the S. P. Railroad.

Facsimile of an ad published throughout 1886 in the San Bernardino Weekly Times supplements.

ern Pacific land grant, as well as many other sections along the 40 mile wide corridor bordering their rail line from Mojave, Kern Co., to The Needles. Although SP has sold much of the original holdings since then, they are still the present largest private land owner in the Mojave Desert.

On April 19, 1883, SP spiked their last rail in place at The Needles where they built a magnificent depot-hotel and other facilities, then they awaited the Atlantic-Pacific arrival from the east.

Calico Junction as it appeared in late 1882. The following year, the town was rechristened Daggett, in honor of California Lieutenant Governor John Daggett, who had local mining interests in the vicinity. *(Pat Keeling — Van Dyke Collection)*

This CSRR time table published shortly after the completion of the route with the A & P main line shows Waterman Junction which was renamed Barstow at the time this ad appeared in the San Bernardino Weekly Times.

(Calico Print, Daggett, CA. Sunday, Feb. 8, 1885, p. 4, c. 2)

Lacking adequate financing and competent leadership, the original A&P went bankrupt in 1875, after building a small portion of their route from Pacific, Kansas, to Vinita, Oklahoma. Here the Indian Territory barred their westward progress. Until 1879 the company receivers did little else but save the A&P from its creditors and form a new company, the St. Louis & San Francisco Railroad, nicknamed the Frisco.

Meanwhile, the twenty year old Atchison, Topeka & Santa Fe Railroad had grown from a mere 50 mile infant to a 900 mile budding transcontinental competitor by the time they reached Santa Fe, New Mexico. Here they found the road west blocked by the pre-empted A&P charter on the 35th parallel.

After negotiations and by January, 1880, Santa Fe had signed two agreements with the Frisco. In the first, they shared jointly all the A&P stocks and control. In the second, called the Tripartite agreement, they revived the A&P unbuilt route from Isleta, New Mexico, to The Needles. This portion, named the A&P Western Division, they pledged to construct and finance in common and to effect independent connections on their own lines.

Although Santa Fe had to assume part of the Frisco liabilities before the partners reached the Colorado River, here only to flounder three months at the crossing, the new A&P rails linked SP steel on August 8, 1883. The first through passenger train left San Francisco, on October 22, 1883.

Great hostility existed between SP, on one hand, and the A&P-Santa Fe combine, on the other. Santa Fe wanted Pacific Coast termini at San Francisco, San Diego and Los Angeles while SP tried to delay them. On the First of October, 1884, SP, having accomplished their objective in securing the land grant on the Mojave to Needles road, leased, with option to buy, their branch line to the A&P. The final purchase deed granted the route to Santa Fe on December 27, 1911 . . . ten months after the completion of the fourth Barstow Harvey House and 27 years since the original lease.

Inching north from San Diego, another Santa Fe enterprise, the California Southern Railroad, finally reached the A&P main line on November 15, 1885. While building their route, the California Southern was authorized a 200 foot right of way. Under the SP lease, this was also the width they were allowed to occupy along the A&P line. Such a corridor was just too narrow for sprawling terminal facilities. After effecting their rail junction close to the Mojave River bridge on SP land, the California Southern settled on the next government land section.

Early in January 1886, they named the station Barstow in honor of William Barstow Strong then Santa Fe's president. They started immediate construction on the eating house-hotel complex.

A photograph shows this very first two story brick building going up. Note the boarding platform made of

William Barstow Strong *(Courtesy of Santa Fe Railway)*

railroad ties and the hastily converted box car used as a depot. The earlier residences hugged the right of way. Had the inhabitants claimed possessory rights? Then how did Santa Fe become the land owner? These are unresolved questions.

Close up of Barstow's first Harvey House. (San Bernardino County Museum — Belden Collection)

Searches through County Archives disclosed a 51.55 acre land development predating the arrival of the California Southern. Mentioned in deeds since 1886, the tract's official map was only recorded in 1901 but under another name. Nine years later it finally appeared on Santa Fe's engineer drawings under its rightful title the Lilienthal subdivision. Besides a few lot proprietors and two tract agents, James Noel and Samuel Dunlap, the original developers were not Barstow residents but lived

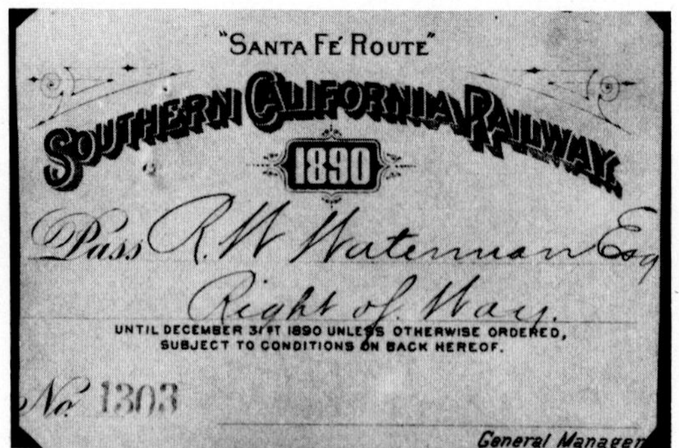

Mojave River Valley Museum *(Drenk Collection)*

QUICK TIME, CHEAP FARES

To Eastern and European Cities

—VIA THE—

Great Trans-continental All-rail Routes,

CENTRAL PACIFIC R. R.

—OR—

SOUTHERN PACIFIC R. R.

Daily Express and Emigrant Trains make prompt connections with the several Railway Lines in the East, connecting at

New York & New Orleans

with the several Steamer Lines to

ALL EUROPEAN PORTS.

PULLMAN PALACE SLEEPING CARS

attached to Overland Express Trains.

THIRD-CLASS SLEEPING CARS

are run daily with Overland Emigrant Trains.

No additional charge for Berths in Third class Cars.

☞ Tickets sold, Sleeping-car Berths secured and other information given upon application at the Company's Offices, where passengers calling in person can secure choice of routes etc

RAILROAD LANDS.

—IN—

NEVADA, CALIFORNIA & TEXAS

FOR SALE ON REASONABLE TERMS.

Apply to, or address,

W. H. MILLS, Land Agent, C. P. R. R. Co., San Francisco,

JEROME MADDEN, Land Agent, S. P R. R. Co., San Francisco, or

H. B. ANDREWS, Land Commissioner G. H. & S. A. Ry. Co., San Antonio, Tex.

A. N. Towne,   T. H. Goodman,

Gen' Manager,   Gen. Pass. & Tkt Agt

SAN FRANCISCO, CAL.

Facsimile of an ad found in the Sunday, February 8, 1885. *(Calico Print, p. 4 c.2)*

Excerpts from the 1888 Santa Fe Official Guide. *(Mojave River Valley Museum — Drenk Collection)*

ATLANTIC & PACIFIC RAILROAD—WESTERN DIVISION.

WESTWARD. No. 1. Pacific Express. Daily.	Distance from Mo. River	STATIONS. See Main Line time table page 9.	EASTWARD. No. 2. Atlantic Express. Daily.
3.20AMWe	887	Lv...........†Albuquerque..........Ar	12.50AM
3.35AM	895	Lv....................Barr..................Ar	12.25AM
3.40 "	897	"....................Isleta................ "	12.20 "
3.50 "	900	"..........A. & P. Junction......... "	12.11AM
4.20 "	*911	"....................Luna................. "	11.45PM
4.45 "	922	"................Rio Puerco........... "	11.15 "
5.20 "	934	"..................San Jose........... "	10.44 "
5.50 "	947	"....................El Rito............. "	10.15 "
6.10 "	953	"...................Laguna............. "	9.55 "
6.25 "	959	"...................Cubero............. "	9.41 "
6.54 "	970	"..................McCartys........... "	9.20 "
7.25 "	983	"....................Grants............. "	8.45 "
7.55 "	994	"..................Bluewater.......... "	8.20 "
8.34AM	1009	Ar..................Chaves............Lv	7.50PM
†9.10AM	1023	Ar...............†Coolidge..........Lv	7.10PM
9.30AM	1023	Lv..................Coolidge.........Ar	†6.45PM
9.51AM	1033	Lv..................Wingate..........Ar	6.20PM
10.17 "	1045	"...................Gallup............. "	5.55 "
10.35 "	1053	"...................Defiance.......... "	5.35 "
10.54 "	1061	"..................Manuelito.......... "	5.12 "
11.20 "	1074	"..................Allantown.......... "	4.41 "
11.50AM	1087	"...................Sanders........... "	4.08 "
12.15PM	1100	"...............Navajo Springs...... "	3.35 "
12.45 "	1113	"...................Billings............ "	3.00 "
1.15 "	1125	"....................Carrizo............ "	2.28 "
1.50 "	1140	"...................Holbrook.......... "	1.50 "
2.15 "	1150	"..................St. Joseph......... "	1.25 "
2.43PM	1161	Ar....................Hardy..............Lv	12.56PM
†3.10PM	1172	Ar..................†Winslow..........Lv	12.30PM
3.45PM	1172	Lv....................Winslow..........Ar	†11.59AM
4.20PM	1185	Lv..................Dennison..........Ar	11.25AM
4.59 "	1198	"...............Canon Diablo......... "	10.55 "
5.44 "	1209	"....................Angell............. "	10.29 "
6.10 "	1215	"...................Walnut............. "	10.15 "
6.25 "	1220	"...................Cosnino............ "	10.03 "
7.15 "	1231	"...................Flagstaff.......... "	9.35 "
7.57 "	1243	"..................Bellemont.......... "	8.55 "
8.40PM	1255	Ar..................Chalender...........Lv	8.18AM
†9.15PM	1265	Ar....................Williams..........Lv	7.45AM
9.45PM	1265	Lv....................Williams..........Ar	†7.15AM
9.54PM	1268	"......................Supai............. "	7.05AM
10.12 "	1273	"...................McLellan........... "	6.43 "
10.31 "	1278	"...................Fairview........... "	6.15 "
11.05 "	1288	"...................Ash Fork.......... "	5.30 "
11.25 "	1296	"...................Pineveta........... "	5.05 "
11.59PM	1306	"...................Crookton........... "	4.35 "
12.25AMTh.	1315	"..............Prescott Junction...... "	4.05 "
12.57 "	1326	"....................Aubrey............ "	3.32 "
1.26AM	1338	"....................Yampal............ "	3.00AM
2.00AM	1352	Ar...........†Peach Springs.........Lv.	2.00AM
2.30AM	1352	Lv............Peach Springs.........Ar.	1.40AM
3.05AM	1364	Lv..................Truxton...........Ar.	12.55AM
3.37 "	1375	"..................Hackberry.......... "	12.10AM
4.15 "	1387	"...................Hualapai........... "	11.30PM
5.00 "	1402	"...................Kingman........... "	10.40 "
5.30 "	1413	"....................Drake............. "	9.35 "
6.08 "	1426	"....................Yucca............. "	8.52 "
6.45 "	1439	"...................Franconia.......... "	8.09 "
7.15AM	1453	"....................Powell............ "	7.28PM
†7.30AM	1461	Ar...........†The Needles..........Lv.	7.00PM
8.00AM	1461	Lv............The Needles..........Ar.	†6.15PM
8.20AM	1468	"......................Java............. "	5.52PM
8.49 "	1475	"......................Ibex............. "	5.32 "
9.21 "	1484	"....................Homer............ "	4.58 "
9.42 "	1492	"....................Goffs............. "	4.27 "
10.02 "	1502	"....................Fenner........... "	3.45 "
10.21 "	1509	"....................Edson............. "	3.12 "
10.42 "	1518	"....................Danby............ "	2.39 "
11.10 "	1531	"....................Cadiz............. "	1.54 "
11.30 "	1539	"....................Bristol........... "	1.27 "
11.45 "	1545	"....................Amboy............ "	1.07 "
11.59AM	1553	Ar..................†Bagdad..........Lv.	12.45 "
12.15PM	1553	Lv....................Bagdad..........Ar.	12.15PM
12.45 "	1560	"....................Siberia........... "	11.50AM
1.29 "	1570	"...................Ash Hill........... "	11.23 "
1.45 "	1577	"....................Ludlow............ "	11.00 "
2.07 "	1586	"....................Lavic............. "	10.32 "
2.30 "	1596	"...................Haslett........... "	10.00 "
3.00 "	1609	"...................Newberry.......... "	9.30 "
3.30 "	1621	"...................Daggett........... "	9.05 "
†3.50PM	1630	Ar....................Barstow..........Lv.	8.45AM
4.30PM	1630	Lv....................Barstow..........Ar.	7.45AM
4.34 "	1641	"...................Waterman.......... "	7.40 "
5.01 "	1640	"...................Hinckley........... "	7.18 "
5.23 "	1650	"....................Harper............ "	6.55 "
5.55 "	1663	"....................Kramer........... "	6.20 "
6.38PM	1681	"....................Rogers............ "	5.35AM
7.30PM	1701	Ar....................Mojave............Lv.	4.45 "

(left margin note) Barstow is the point on MAIN LINE (A. & P. R.R.) where passengers, through or to Southern California, take the California Southern Line. See Map.

(right margin note) Mojave is junction point on Southern Pacific R. R. for passengers who do not go by the way of Southern California. See Barstow as above, and map.

CALIFORNIA SOUTHERN R. R.—BARSTOW DIVISION.

Time changes One Hour.

SOUTHWARD No. 39. Daily.	No. 1. Daily.	Miles	STATIONS.	NORTHWARD No. 2. Daily.	No. 38. Daily.
5.20 AM	3.30PMTh	1630	Lv...............Barstow...........Ar.	6.30AMTh	11.30 AM
6.05 "	3.49 "	1642	"............Cottonwood.......... "	6.05	10.50 "
6.38 "	4.04 "	1651	"...........Point of Rocks........ "	5.45	10.17 "
7.18 "	4.21 "	1661	"............Oro Grande.......... "	5.24	9.42 "
8.00 "	4.34 "	1667	"..............Victor............ "	5.13	9.22 "
8.42 "	4.59 "	1675	"..............Hesperia.......... "	4.53	8.42 "
9.42 "	5.30 "	1686	"..............Summit........... "	4.28	7.47 "
10.12 "	6.07 "	1692	"...............Cajon............ "	3.53	6.47 "
11.07 "	6.37 "	1703	"..............Irvington.......... "	3.05	5.42 "
11.42 AM	6.55PM	1711	Ar...........†San Bernardino......Lv.	2.45AM	5.10 AM

BARSTOW TO LOS ANGELES, SAN DIEGO AND NATIONAL CITY.

	Miles	STATIONS.		
3.30 PMTh	1647	Lv.......Barstow.......Ar.	Cal. So'n	6 30AMTu
4.34 "	1654	Lv.........Victor........ "		5.13 "
6.55 "	1728	Ar...†San Bernardino..Lv.		2.45 "
7.20 PM	1728	Lv...San Bernardino..Ar.	Cal. Cent.	12.45AMTu
9.36 PM	1787	Ar......Los Angeles....Lv.		10.00PM Mo.
10.37 PMTh	1787	Lv......Los Angeles....Ar.	Cal. Cent.	9.24 PMMo
12.05 AMFr	1821	"........Santa Ana...... "		7.54 "
12.56 "	1846	"........San Juan....... "		7.08 "
1.53 "	1870	"....Los Angeles June.. "		6.11 "
2.01 "	1872	"........Oceanside...... "	Cal. So'n	6 06 "
4.01 "	1913	"........San Diego...... "		4.00 "
4.21 AM	1918	Ar....National City...Lv.		3.30 PMMo

BARSTOW TO SAN FRANCISCO AND PORTLAND. "THE MT. SHASTA ROUTE."

	Miles	STATIONS.		
4.30 PMTh	1647	Lv......Barstow......Ar.	At. & Pac	7.45 AMTu
7.30 "	1718	Ar......†Mojave......Lv.	"	4.45 "
7.20 "	1718	Lv......Mojave......Ar.	So. Pac.	2.25 "
9.20 "	1750	Ar.......Keene........ "	"	12.25 AMTu
11.45 "	1786	"........Sumner....... "	"	10.15 PM
1.55 AM Fr	1849	Lv.......Tulare.......Lv.	"	8.10 "
4.42 "	1922	Ar.......Berenda....... "	"	4.53 "
7.02 "	1986	Lv.......Modesto...... "	"	2.31 "
8.20 "	2006	Lv.......Lathrop....... "	"	1.50 "
8.45 "	2017	Ar........Tracy........ "	"	1.05 PM
12.15 PM Fr	2100	Ar...San Francisco..Lv.	"	9.30 AMMo
7.00 P.M	2100	Lv...San Francisco..Ar.	So. Pac.	7.45 AM
10.40 "	2190	Ar.....Sacramento....Lv.	"	3.55 "
11.00 P.M	2190	Lv.....Sacramento....Ar.	"	3.40 AMMo
4.10AMSat	2313	Ar.......Tehama......Lv.	"	10.05 PM
6.30 "	2360	"........Redding....... "	"	7.55 "
11.15 A.M	2438	"........Sisson........ "	"	3.19 P.M
5.10 P.M	2531	"........Ashland....... "	"	9.00 AMSu
8.45 AMSu	2792	"........Albany........ "	"	7.45 P.M
10.40 AM	2872	Ar......Portland.....Lv.	"	4.00PMSat

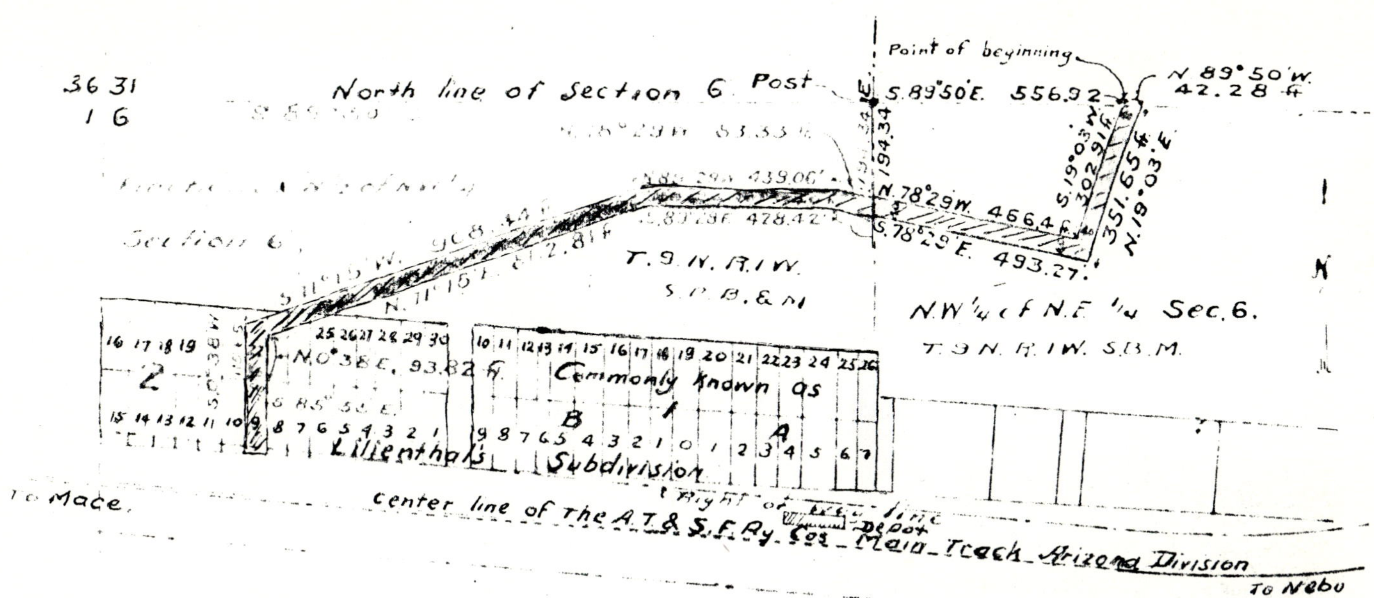

A composite of 1910's Santa Fe Engineer drawings originally appended to two deeds granting a new street (shaded) to San Bernardino County. It is the only document known to show Barstow's Lilienthal Subdivision by name. Willow Street (between block 1 and 2) was pre-empted by the 1910-11 construction of the Casa del Desierto and new passenger tracks. Notice that Elm Street right-of-way is altogether missing from this blueprint. *(San Bernardino County Archives — Moon collection)*

in New York and San Francisco.

In 1880, at the time James Noel claimed mining interests in the Mojave District, the Lilienthal family made history in the Jewish annals by signing the famous "Lilienthal Family Pact", whereby they pooled their assets to further joint enterprises. The pact's seven signers were the sons of two very prominent Jewish brothers, natives of Munich, Germany. Amongst other vocations, their businesses were banking, merchandising agricultural products, real estate and the wholesale of whiskey, their brand being "Crown Distilleries". In the Mojave Desert they were liquor license bondmen, "booze" wholesalers and landlords at Barstow.

Early local news is scarce . . . Business thrived at the first Barstow eating house as waves of excursionists swarmed to Southern California. These excursionists, often prospective emigrants from the East, responded to the advertising campaigns waged by land schemers, and these were plentiful. From the West, passengers were generally people on the way to visit their old home. Both groups just passed through. Locally, the passengers were mostly Calico residents traveling West or South for business and pleasure. They had discovered that they could save money by buying round trip tickets at Barstow, instead of getting the one way fare available at Daggett. The station was serviced by the Livingstone & Cahill Stage with headquarters at Calico and Barstow.

West of Albuquerque, the SP, A&P and California Southern railroads had eight depot-hotel-eating houses: five situated in California at Needles, Barstow, San Bernardino, Mojave and Lathrop; two located in Arizona at Williams and Winslow; the last being at Coolidge, New Mexico. All these eating houses, (that is, the business proper as opposed to the structures which belonged to the railroad) were owned by Stackpole & Lincoln, the western forerunners of Fred Harvey.

LOW RATE EXCURSION TICKETS

At "One Fare for the Round Trip," to Points in Kansas, Indian Territory, Texas (via Purcell), Pan Handle of Texas, and Colorado east of and including La Junta. Tickets will be on Sale October 9th and October 23d, and will be limited to 30 days, with Stop-over privileges West-Bound only.

EXCURSION TICKETS TO LAS VEGAS, N. M.

Will be on Sale October 3d, 9th, 17th, 23d, November 7th, 21st, and December 5th. Tickets will be limited to 60 days. Going and returning limit, 15 days each. Stop-over privileges allowed.

STOP-OVER Privileges will be given to holders of ROUND TRIP OR EXCURSION TICKETS

To COLORADO, NEW MEXICO and CALIFORNIA POINTS; also on first-class unlimited tickets, and on first-class limited tickets within their time limits, upon request at the time of presenting tickets on our trains.

This ad appeared on page 25 of the 1888 Santa Fe Official Guide. note that Fred Harvey is not mentioned as the proctor of the route's Eating Houses *(Mojave River Valley Museum — Drenk Collection)*

S. P. and A. & P. and C. S. Railroad

EATING HOUSES,

STACKPOLE & LINCOLN, Prop's.

First-class in every detail, and tables supplied with every delicacy the markets afford.

Lathrop Hotel, Lathrop; Depot Hotel, San Bernardino; Depot Hotel, Mojave; Barstow Hotel, Barstow; Needles House, Needles, Cal; Williams House, Williams, Arizona; Winslow House, Winslow, Arizona; Coolidge House, Coolidge, New Mexico.

(Facsimile of advertisement found in Weekly Times supplement, San Bernardino, April 16, 1887—p.5, c.4)

A late 1887 view of Barstow. In the mid background Buzzard Rock looms in the dry bed of the Mojave River; on the south bank of the river, the businesses and residential center are strung along Elm Street. Note the Gooding complex north of the railroad's coal chutes (elevated tracks). The depot (second) and Harvey House are located between the tracks to the right of the photo. Observe the "pagoda hip roofs" on these buildings; especially on the eastern addition to the hotel. In the foreground the crude turntable is flanked by locomotives. The water tower supplying the facilities is on the lower right of the photo. *(Gooding-Mitchell Collection)*

In May, 1887, the Santa Fe-Fred Harvey forces slowly squeezed them out of business, first by taking over the San Bernardino, Barstow and Needles houses, second by splitting the original owners' holdings. Early that year, Stackpole & Lincoln had suffered "tremendous losses by fire" when suddenly banks foreclosed on their mortgaged furnishings while clients withheld payment of bills.

Now, let's highlight Frederick Henry Harvey's career.

Byron Harvey, Jr., President of Fred Harvey System in 1946, grandson of Fred Harvey. Started to work in Harvey System in 1928 as retail clerk in drug store at the Chicago Union Station. *(Addie Bassett Collection)*

Frederick Henry Harvey — 1835-1901 *(Photo courtesy of Santa Fe Railway)*

Born in London, June 27, 1835, he sailed from Liverpool to New York where, at barely fifteen, he landed his first restaurant job. Following similar employment at New Orleans, he moved to St. Louis in 1855 where, with a partner, he opened his own restaurant. This venture closed at the onset of the Civil War.

At twenty-four, he wed a Bohemian girl from Prague, Barbara Sarah Mattas, nicknamed Sally. This life long partner gave him five living children. Sibyl, Minnie and Marie were the girls, Ford and Byron were the boys. At their father's death, February 9, 1901, Ford and Byron ran the Fred Harvey System and brought the company to peak efficiency. They successfully established, under Santa Fe's lease, the modern and elegant hotels later built throughout the Southwest.

After the Civil War, Fred Harvey worked first as a postal clerk, then traffic manager, and finally as traveling agent for mid-west railroads. He started with the Hannibal & St. Joseph, in Kansas, ending his railroad career in 1882 while employed by the Chicago, Burlington & Quincy, in Illinois. Meanwhile, from 1875 and 1882, he moonlighted and re-entered his restaurateur trade at Hugo and Wallace, Kansas, where a partner ran the business for him; this lasted a year.

Fred Harvey was familiar with the food and service offered at railroad eating houses. These dingy beaneries slung unfit "edibles" and peddled "railroader's pies" consisting of stale sandwiches and coffee. From personal experiences, he conceived an idea to provide tastier meals, better service and cleaner surroundings for employees and passengers alike. He believed that railroads themselves would gain popularity and customers by cooperating with his project. He first approached the Burlington management by asking for a lease of all the eating houses which he would run under his general management. They rebuffed him, jokingly suggesting that he try the venturesome Santa Fe. Being progressive and strongly competitive, Santa Fe accepted with reservations. In 1876, the joint experiment started in the old Topeka station, and soon was followed by a second Harvey House at Florence, Kansas. Both places were esthetically a far cry from the later edifices gracing the Santa Fe Route from Chicago to Los Angeles. The quarters were clean, attractively decorated and served family style meals. Fresh table linen from Ireland and shining silver from England gave a touch of class to the establishments. The real magnet bewitching country folks, tourists and railroaders alike, was the young, single and well trained "Kansas" waitress, the Harvey Girl . . . She

A late 1892, or later view of Barstow. The original eastbound tracks rounded Stockyards Hill (right background) on the south bank of the Mojave River. Along Elm Street businesses and residences have increased as well as the rail yards. The turn table, still in existence, would be located out and to left in the photo. New houses have sprouted on the side of the railroad. Note the newly graded Cottage Street. *(Martha Burnau Collection)*

and her sisters migrated West as Harvey Houses proliferated at the same rate of growth as its parent, the Santa Fe; in the unsettled wilds, stewards replaced the Harvey Girls.

On July 8, 1887, the first Barstow Harvey House and depot burned. The San Bernardino Weekly Times published the story of the week old event in its July 16th Saturday edition as follows:

The Fire at Barstow

Passengers coming in from Barstow this morning give the following account of the fire that destroyed the depot hotel at that place yesterday. One gentleman especially, who appears to have made a thorough investigation of the matter says: "The fire was first discovered in the laundry room, but it originated under the platform. The sparks from engine No. 40, fell through the cracks in the platform, and caught in the shaving, and other debris. Things were so dry that the flames spread like a hurricane and inside of five minutes the entire building was in flames. The men around the depot did all they could to subdue the flames, but their efforts were simply thrown away. Then all hands went to work taking the tables out of the dining room. Most of the things were removed from the dining room, but that was about all that was saved. The building, as near as I could learn, cost in the neighborhood of seventeen thousand dollars, and the platform and other losses will bring the total loss close up to $22,000. The building belonged to the California Southern road and was fully insured. The dining room was run by Fred Harvey, whose loss will not be very heavy. When we left there it was understood that the building would be rebuilt at once; in fact workmen were being engaged to go to work on Monday morning cleaning away the debris."

Until the depot at Barstow is repaired, the passengers coming this way will take their meals at San Bernardino. There were no lives lost, the report to the contrary not withstanding.

In another column the reporter wrote:

"Blackie White, one of the engineers on the California Southern was at the fire at Barstow the other day, and the steward of the hotel told him that he left a small amount of silver in the safe, as it got too hot for him when he was taking the money out. Blackie rolled up his sleeves and dashed into the flames and smoke and in a few seconds came rushing out with a dollar and a half in his hands. He was black as a coon and as he emerged the crowd gave him a round of applause. The money was voted to him for his bravery."

Barstow depot built in late 1887. *(San Bernardino County Museum — Belden Collection)*

This 1887 view of Leonard Gooding General Store, on the right, shows the temporary railroad facilities at Barstow which he managed during the construction of the second Harvey House. He stands on the right with his family. *(Martha Burnau Collection)*

The above appears on page 25 of the 1888 Santa Fe Official Guide
(Mojave River Valley Museum — Drenk Collection)

These three photos picture the successive alterations made by Santa Fe between 1892 and 1908 on their passenger facilities at Barstow. This (third) Harvey House exhibits nine windows on the hotel upper floor. Note the new southern extension of the pedestrian viaduct and the additional floor above the depot (building in the middle of the complex). Tentative dates for the photographs are 1902 for the first one, and 1905 for the others. *(Top: Mojave River Valley Museum — Payne Collection; the others: Martha Burnau Collection)*

The Weekly Times reporter was right. Fred Perris, Chief Engineer for the California Southern, had a plumber busy laying water pipes by August. On September 20, 1887, Perris signed a $17,500 contract with

The Ibsen photo taken in June 23, 1911, shows Santa Fe workers mopping up after the 4 a.m. conflagration which destroyed the old frame roundhouse, the wooden shops and 16 locomotives at Barstow. The loss was estimated at $450,000.00. *(Pat Keeling — Wm. Smart Collection).* (Lower photo). On the right the newly constructed railroad facilities fill the edge of the tracks. *(Martha Burnau Collection)*

On November 23, 1910, at 11:30 A.M., Barstow shook when a terrific explosion went off in the East Cut. The force of the blast threw legs, arms and mangled bodies in all directions. The corpse of a Mexican was recovered above and 250 feet away from the Cut. Four men were killed instantly, possibly two others died in Los Angeles where two more lay critically wounded. Eight victims in all. To comment on our historic past . . . newsmen reflected the bigoted attitude of their times by seldom using the given names of either Mexicans, Orientals, Indians or Blacks. This was the case in the article mentioned above, when even in death, five Mexicans remained nameless.

At the coroner's inquest, the jurors were some railroad men, Barstow's undertakers, and a member of the contracting firm. Their verdict was "death caused by an accidental and premature explosion of dynamite with no blame attached to any individual or parties". But another story was told by the Old Calico powdermen, who had worked for the contractor, and quit because of the unsafe job requirements.

In May, 1910, the Case del Desierto walls emerged from the land fill. Designed by a woman architect, Mary Colter, the reinforced concrete and brick structure was

Pedro Duran and an unidentified man pose inside the Barstow Machine Shop tool room in 1918. *(Mojave River Valley Museum — Duran Collection)*

to host a multitude of services, primarily for Santa Fe employees and railroad passengers. It was almost a self-contained little city, and the fifth luxurious edifice built west of Albuquerque.

The pseudo Spanish-Moroccan complex revolutionized the otherwise styleless Barstow landscape, being admirably suited for the desert. It displayed a far superior architectural design than its earlier Neo-Roman counterpart at Needles.

This spring of 1910 photo reproduction courtesy of Santa Fe Railway, is the best overview record of Barstow at the time the railraod undertook its major construction projects completing them by the end of 1912. Note the original roundhouse on the right background and the crane-like tower (on the left) standing on the future site of the Casa del Desierto. Observe the westerly residential tents.

1911. Assembled fresno teams awaiting the day's orders. Shown on the right background is the roundhouse which burned that year. The lighter brick structure with chimneys (middle) is the newly constructed power house. (Photo, San Bernardino County

The Mojave River flood of Jan 1, 1910. The building on the foreground was D.C. Henderson's Department Store. Appended to it was the post office at the corner of Elm and Willow Streets. Next was the Fletcher Theater, then the Inez Hotel. (Photo, San

A violent desert flash flood surges with destructive force northward across Santa Fe tracks before reaching Old Town at the other end of the viaduct. *(Rex Dillingham Collection)*

This 1910 view of Barstow freight and passenger yards dimly show construction crew excavating the slope of Stockyards Hill for the future East Cut where Santa Fe rerouted their eastbound tracks, thus eliminating a dangerous bend on the north of the hill. *(Rex Dillingham Collection)*

The Barstow complex was actually divided into three main buildings all interconnected by graceful covered walkways and shaded by spacious verandas. The western area encompassed the Santa Fe workmen's home, called the "Reading Room". In this tri-level affair, day sleeping quarters occupied the second floor while the dormitory took up the basement. The main floor contained the manager's or housekeeper's office, a library and a recreation hall furnished with bookcases, card and game tables. Furthermore, the Barstow Printer of February 17, 1911, reported that the "rec. hall" had a bowling alley, pool and billiard tables.

Santa Fe doctors moved the medical offices into the east portion of the recreation room in 1926. Previously it had doubled as a theatre showing free monthly Santa Fe sponsored entertainment for railroad employees and town residents alike. The theater groups, whether chautauqua players, acrobat, magician or vocal performers, traveled from one main station to the next, much to the enjoyment of everyone. In the early 1930's, the traveling shows appeared less often, then came only once a year. These later performances were held at the Waterman School auditorium. By World War II, they stopped altogether.

The lawn facing the Reading Room was protected on either end by covered walkways leading to the brick walk at the tracks edge. The grassy plot was divided by a pergola clothed with flowering bushes. Many veteran Harvey Girls and retired railroad men, with a twinkle in their eyes, recall this sheltered arbor where they could whisper sweet words on romantic evenings.

At the southwest end of the lawn, a small outpost housed the "Santa Fe bull", special detective, and also served to store carmen supplies and ice. This building was demolished in 1976. The Reading Room fell earlier when the whole western portion was razed, although it had been leased since 1947.

The central part of the complex bordering the tracks was the depot, now used by Amtrak since May, 1971. In 1911 this building contained the waiting room, ticket office, baggage room and the Wells, Fargo & Co. Office. This company later was replaced by the Railway Express.

The eastern part of the complex, presently vacant and a haven for pigeons, was the hotel-restaurant proper, the heart of the Casa del Desierto. This fourth Barstow Harvey House opened without fanfare or celebration on Washington's Birthday, February 22, 1911,

A 1910 winter view of the Casa del Desierto complex: (L to R) the "Reading Room", the depot and hotel-restaurant. In front of the buildings, note the workers setting the brick pavement and the stacked ties ready for use in the construction of the seven passenger tracks. In the mid-foreground stands "Old Town" bordered by Elm Street. The Barstow Ice Plant, managed by E.L. Mudgett, which supplied ice and the first electric power to the residents is on the extreme left. On the right is the north end of the pedestrian viaduct over the busy freight yards. north of the Casa del Desierto "Buzzard Rock" guards the Mojave River bridge; note the homesteads behind. *(Photo courtesy of Santa Fe Railway)*

This Gay Hamilton photograph reproduction, courtesy of Santa Fe Railway, was originally published in the August, 1911, issue of Santa Fe Magazine. It portrays the first Casa del Desierto manager, Carl Rummick, seated on the extreme left and his staff. In 1900, Mr. Rummick was the cashier at the Bagdad Harvey House. It is believed the ladies in the center row were laundresses. The gong attendant is recognized by his derby hat, the porters by their caps.

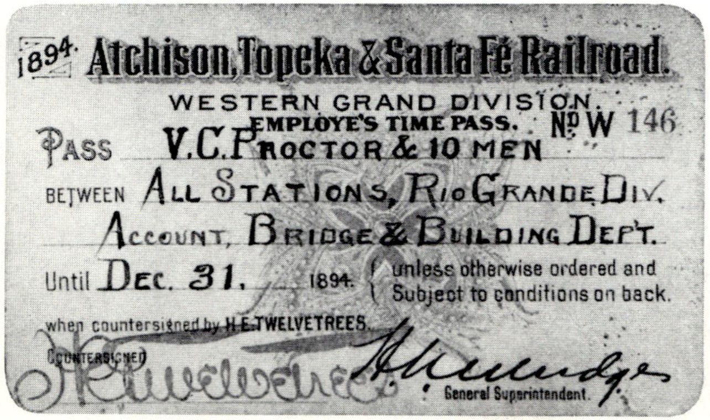

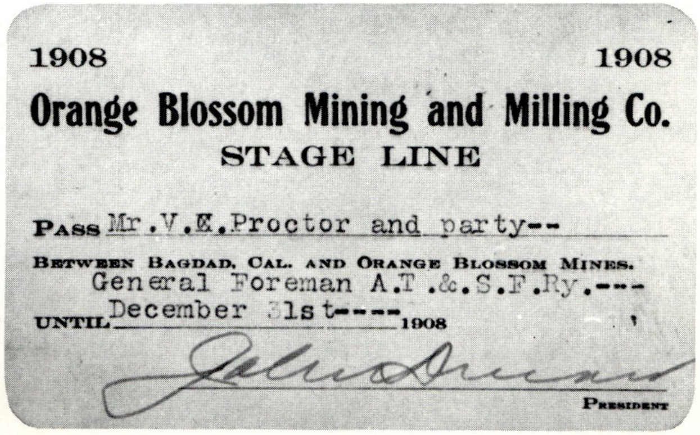

1908   1908

Orange Blossom Mining and Milling Co.

STAGE LINE

Pass Mr. V. E. Proctor and party--

Between Bagdad, Cal. and Orange Blossom Mines.

General Foreman A.T.&S.F. Ry. --

Until, December 31st---- 1908

[signature] President

(Pattison Collection)

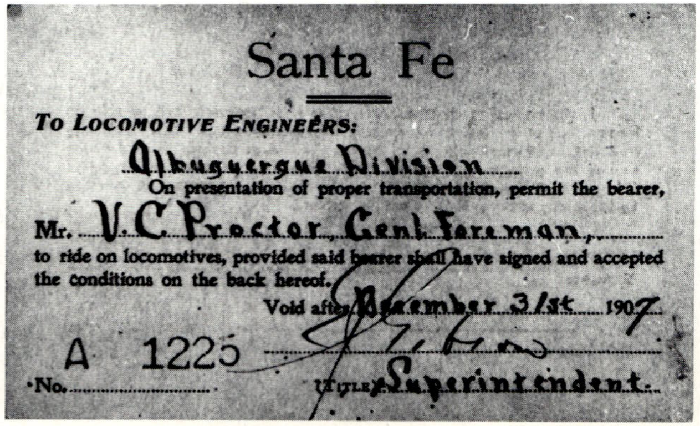

Santa Fe

To Locomotive Engineers:

Albuquerque Division

On presentation of proper transportation, permit the bearer,

Mr. V.C. Proctor, Genl. Foreman,

to ride on locomotives, provided said license that have signed and accepted the conditions on the back hereof. Void after December 31st 1907

A 1225

No. [signature] Acg'g Superintendent.

(Pattison Collection)

Atchison, Topeka & Santa Fe Railroad.

WESTERN GRAND DIVISION

EMPLOYEE'S TIME PASS. No W 146.

Pass V.C. Proctor & 10 men

Between All Stations, Rio Grande Div.

Account Bridge & Building Dept.

Until Dec. 31. 1894. unless otherwise ordered and Subject to conditions on back.

when countersigned by H.E. TWELVETREES.

COUNTERSIGNED [signature] General Superintendent.

(Pattison Collection)

A late 1920's view of the pergola fronting Santa Fe Reading Room which housed the railroad employees *(Addie Bassett Collection)*

A 1978 view of Barstow's Amtrack Office which opens only for a short time twice a day. *(David Ottalini photo — Barstow Harvey House Society Collection)*

Barstow Harvey House manager, Eddie Behean and family in the front of the Casa del Desierto in 1931. *(Addie Bassett Collection)*

soon after the eastbound "Tourist Flyer" pulled into the station at 1:40 P.M. During the next 40 minutes, manager Carl Rummich and his staff served the first patrons in both dining room and at the lunch counter. Since the previous December, railroad employees had moved throughout other parts of the complex.

In the lobby, majestic stairs led to the 25 guest rooms upstairs where Harvey House managers luxuriated in a four bedroom apartment side by side with transient railroad officials and customers. In the corner of the lobby, an independent Fred Harvey enterprise peddled everything from sandwiches to magazines and souvenirs at the news stand, a service similar to our present airport gift shops. During World War II, in order to reduce the congestion inside, the news stand was moved into the northwestern corner of the dining room addition. This addition, built in November, 1943, enclosed the original dining room veranda on two sides to provide space for long tables needed to seat a multitude of hungry G.I.'s.

The horseshoe lunch counter, kitchen and bakery area occupied the left side of the lobby, the dining room being on the right. The total seating accommodations were for 120 persons. In May, 1943, manager Irvin Krause distinguished himself by establishing the first 24 hour self-service cafeteria in the Harvey House System. Here, he fed exclusively Santa Fe employees, even posting a guard outside to keep the public away. Krause's reward was a 1945 transfer to the beautiful Alvarado Hotel at Albuquerque where he died in March, 1947.

SANTA FE MEAL SERVICE
(Management Fred Harvey)

The dining-car, dining-room, and hotel service of the Santa Fe is managed by Fred Harvey. It is the best railway meal service in the world. All through passenger trains, which do not carry dining cars, are scheduled to stop at dining stations, placed at convenient points along the line. *Ample time is allowed for meals.*

All dining cars are equipped with electric lights and electric fans. A ventilating device in the kitchen removes all odor of cooking. Meals a la carte, except that on the California Limited the dinners are table d'hote.

Below is given a list of stations at which dining rooms and lunch rooms will be found:

DINING ROOMS	DINING ROOMS	DINING ROOMS
Albuquerque, N. M.	La Junta, Colo.	Wellington, Kan.
Amarillo, Tex.	Lamy, N. M.	Williams, Ariz.
Arkansas City, Kan.	Las Vegas, N. M.	Winslow, Ariz.
Ash Fork, Ariz.	Merced, Cal.	Ferry Steamers "San
Bakersfield, Cal.	Needles, Cal.	Pablo" and "San
Barstow, Cal.	Newton, Kan.	Pedro," San Francisco.
Clovis, N. M.	Purcell, Okla.	
Dallas, Tex.	Rincon, N. M.	Dearborn Station,
Deming, N. M.	Syracuse, Kan.	Chicago, and Union
Dodge City, Kan.	Temple, Tex.	Depot restaurant,
Emporia, Kan.	Topeka, Kan.	El Paso, are also
Gallup, N. M.	Trinidad, Colo.	managed by Fred
Hutchinson, Kan.	Waynoka, Okla.	Harvey.

LUNCH ROOMS	LUNCH ROOMS	LUNCH ROOMS
Albuquerque, N. M.	Guthrie, Okla.	Somerville, Texas.
Amarillo, Tex.	Hutchinson, Kan.	Temple, Texas.
Arkansas City, Kan.	Kingman, Ariz.	Topeka, Kan.
Ash Fork, Ariz.	La Junta, Colo.	Trinidad, Colo.
Bakersfield, Cal.	Lamy, N. M.	Vaughn, N. M.
Barstow, Cal.	Las Vegas, N. M.	Waynoka, Okla.
Belen, N. M.	Los Angeles, Cal.	Wellington, Kan.
Canadian, Texas	Merced, Cal.	Williams, Ariz.
Chanute, Kan.	Mojave, Cal.	Winslow, Ariz.
Cleburne, Texas.	Needles, Cal.	Ferry Steamers "San
Clovis, N. M.	Newton, Kan.	Pablo" and "San
Colorado Springs, Colo.	Purcell, Okla.	Pedro," San Francisco.
Dallas, Tex.	Rincon, N. M.	
Deming, N. M.	Rosenberg, Texas.	Dearborn Station restaurant, Chicago,
Dodge City, Kan.	Syracuse, Kan.	Union Depot restaurant, El Paso, and
Emporia, Kan.	San Bernardino, Cal	
Gallup, N. M.	San Marcial, N. M.	Union Station Lunch
Gainesville, Texas.	Seligman, Ariz.	Room, Houston.
Galveston, Texas.	Silsbee, Texas.	

Hotel Accommodations are provided at:

Albuquerque, N. M.	La Junta, Colo.	Seligman, Ariz.
Ash Fork, Ariz.	Lamy, N. M.	Syracuse, Kan.
Barstow, Cal.	Las Vegas, N. M.	Temple, Tex.
Clovis, N. M.	Mojave, Cal.	Trinidad, Colo.
Deming, N. M.	Needles, Cal.	Vaughn, N. M.
Dodge City, Kan.	Newton, Kan.	Wellington, Kan.
Emporia, Kan.	Rincon, N. M.	Williams, Ariz.
Grand Canyon, Ariz.	San Marcial, N. M.	Winslow, Ariz.
Hutchinson, Kan.		

The most noteworthy of the Santa Fe hotels are:

THE BISONTE, at Hutchinson, Kan., with 67 guest rooms and dining room seats for 120.

THE SEQUOYAH, at Syracuse, Kan., with 16 guest rooms and a dining room seating 100.

GRAN QUIVIRA, at Clovis, N. M., has 25 guest rooms and dining accommodations for 75 persons.

LOS CHAVES, at Vaughn, N. M., with 10 guest rooms and a dining room seating 42 persons.

THE CARDENAS, at Trinidad, Colo., with 37 guest rooms and a dining room with seats for 108.

THE CASTAÑEDA, at Las Vegas, N. M., has 43 guest rooms and dining accommodations for about 100.

EL ORTIZ, at Lamy, N. M., is unique. Designed especially for those who stop over to visit old Santa Fé.

THE ALVARADO, at Albuquerque, N. M., with 70 guest rooms and dining accommodations for 160. The famous Fred Harvey Indian Museum is located here.

THE FRAY MARCOS, at Williams, Ariz., is an adjunct to El Tovar at the Grand Canyon.

EL TOVAR, at Grand Canyon, which is described in detail on another page.

THE ESCALANTE, at Ash Fork, Ariz., with 31 guest rooms and a dining room seating 120.

EL GARCES, at Needles, Cal., has 65 guest rooms and dining accommodations for twice that number.

CASA DEL DESIERTO, at Barstow, Cal., has 25 guest rooms and dining accommodations for about 120.

"The most noteworthy Santa Fe hotels" noted above were the company's new edifices geared to the interest of the tourists. Santa Fe Official Guide printed in November 20, 1911, p. 94. *(Mojave River Valley Museum — Drenk Collection)*

GIs and train crew patronizing Barstow's Harvey System Newsstand in 1943. *(Addie Bassett Collection)*

These two early 1920's interior views of the Casa del Desierto show almost the full extent of the room as it originally stood. Each table accommodates 8 patrons, the maximum seating capacity being for 104 persons. Note the old fashioned side board along the eastern wall and the Christmas table arrangements (bottom). The eating pass (middle) is a very rare collector's item. In order to be served in the dining room, male customers had to wear coat and ties. This was not mandatory in the lunchroom. *(Top photo: Addie Bassett Collection. Bottom photo: Garland Dittman Collection. Middle: Pattison Collection)*

The top photograph depicts the Casa del Desierto horse-shoe lunch counter in 1922. Note Fred Harvey Newsstand display in the background, the frieze details around the walls and the beautiful copper chandelier. This latter item was sold, along with other furnishings, at the closure of the Harvey House. In December 1943, Santa Fe Magazine published the photo below with an accompanying story. It expounded Fred Harvey's "newest wartime endeavor" as manager Irvin G. Krause innovated the first "around the clock self service facilities" in the old Barstow lunchroom the previous May. The new cafeteria "met with such instant success" that similar arrangements followed at the Needles and Seligman Houses. It was set up for the sole use of railroad men on duty and a guard, posted outside, kept the public out. That year the dining room seating capacity was increased by enclosing the eastern half of the veranda in order to serve the endless flow of troops. *(Addie Bassett Collection)*

From the central "food preparation room", the back of the Harvey House ended in two wings. A short hall led to an L-shaped dormitory on the west; the male help lodged in the basement while Harvey Girls shared rooms on the first floor. The second floor, reserved for guests and railroaders, joined the seventeen rooms above the restaurant.

1926 view of the food preparation area at Vaugh, N.M. At Barstow the room was very similar although larger. Note the steam table on the right *(Addie Bassett Collection)*

View of the northeast wing of the Casa del Desierto. A loading dock lined the lower building which originally contained the laundry, ice plant, cool storage lockers, bottling plant, etc. Harvey Girl, Jessie Park and the manager's wife, Mrs. Behean, are enjoying a game of tennis. *(Addie Bassett Collection)*

The northeast wing, a multi-purpose area, contained the staff lunchroom, offices, storage and processing facilities. It was serviced by a side track where box cars, backed along the loading dock, discharged staple goods, meat, fresh produce and other cargoes. At one time it housed the commissary, ice cream plant, ice making and crushing facilities, butchering station and the laundry. A 1931 Harvey House staff photograph shows, back in the 3rd row and proudly wearing a "K" on his T-shirt, Orville Lewis. For six years (1931-36), Orville made at least one daily batch of ice cream with a machine whose top capacity was 30 gallons. A few times, he produced as high as 50 gallons daily. Flavors were varied: vanilla, chocolate, strawberry, peppermint and even raisin, just to name a few. Many enterprising youths earned pocket money by peddling, on commission, the frozen delicacy as well as an orange drink, at train arrivals.

1931 Barstow Harvey House Crew. Eddie Behean, manager. *(Addie Bassett Collection, from an original Santa Fe Railway photo)*

Sometimes the job became a family trade as each boy passed the concession to his next younger brother, and so on . . . Besides being sold locally, the ice cream was supplied to some dining cars and to other Harvey Houses such as Needles, Seligman, Winslow, San Bernardino and even Los Angeles and San Diego.

Marring the landscape, a huge round water tower loomed behind the Harvey House. Speaking of water, originally the complex sewer pipes discharged their poison directly into the Mojave River, a common practice at that time.

In the 1920's Santa Fe strived for the consolidation of their passenger and freight yards, the sole obstacle being the narrow strip of land left in between the two — Old Town. Petty annoyances started over the street right of way, fire protection and, with the increase of automobile traffic, the constant blockage of the highway crossing. To add to the tension, the town constable also served as the Santa Fe bull. The fire protection crew, an all volunteer effort of Santa Fe employees manning a specially equipped locomotive, seemed slow in responding to emergencies. Finally the railway company pushed for re-

Early pop corn, peanut, refreshment and ice cream vendor at San Bernardino Depot. *(San Bernardino County Museum — Belden Collection)*

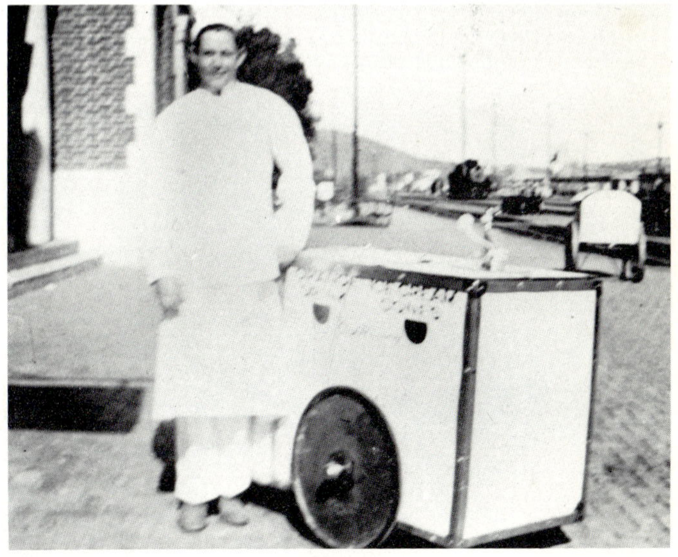

1940. Willis Pinkerton, shown here, was the last ice cream and orange drink "platform" vendor for Fred Harvey at Barstow. Two Willis brothers, Richard and Al, preceeded Pinkerton in that job. *(Willis Pinkerton Collection)*

It seems unlikely that while planning their new 1910 depot, Santa Fe didn't foresee the eventual condemnation of "Old Town". They encircled with raised tracks all the business section allowing only a mandatory highway crossing and pedestrian viaduct. At the opening of the Harvey House, they issued a warning to property owners asking them to "clean up and make presentable the yards facing the station" and "to fence objectionable features". Whether or not the residents complied is unknown but the tall fence abutting the north perimeter of Old Town prevented pedestrian traffic into the passenger yards and served as an earth retaining wall. It isolated the railroad passengers from the town business center and vice-versa. During prohibition, audacious law breakers loosened a few boards, thus preparing their getaway route well in advance of the sheriff's raids.

June 11, 1921. Fire racing through the Barstow Hotel and Melrose Hotel. Fighting the blaze is the specially equipped Santa Fe locomotive sidetracked west of the freight office. *(Rex Dillingham Collection)*

The Mojave River rampaging through North Barstow Addition in 1938. Fifteen years earlier some residents had relocated here after vacating Old Town. After the flood many joined their friends "uptown" in the vicinity of Main Street. *(Left: C. Mitchell Collection. Right: R. Stapp Collection)*

The westbound "California Limited" poses at Barstow in the late 1920's. Note metal wheels on the baggage carts. After WWII, these were replaced and fitted with tires. Northeastward view of the Casa del Desierto and the passenger yards, late 1930's. *(Left: Courtesy of Santa Fe Railway. Right: Agnes Copp Collection)*

location of the residents, but haggles over property values and the uncertain ultimate location of the long overdue highways impeded the concerned parties. Then, Santa Fe offered lots on the present Main Street in exchange for Old Town properties plus, they indemnified the owners, helping them to move entire business buildings up the hill. Condemnation procedures started against the last three business owners who settled out of court in 1927.

Contrary to published literature, the "famous" Harvey service was only as good as its local management and dishonesty existed . . . Fred Harvey Company did not acquire all its assets on "a hand shake contract" nor by "running the business regardless of cost". Meals were fairly expensive at the depots as well as in the dining cars; consequently town competitors were eliminated by fencing in the modern Harvey Houses.

Soldiers and flat cars loaded with cannons westbound. (World War I)

Red Cross Volunteers on Armistice Day at Barstow.

Red Cross ladies giving lunch baskets to hungry troops on board westbound train during World War I. *(Photos: Mojave River Valley Museum — Pauline Carter Collection)*

Unknown and Della Cameron Carter, Harvey Girls at Barstow before WWI. Note the white uniform used during summer, the black dress in winter. *(Jean Phee Lundgren Collection)*

Mary Ryan, head waitress at Barstow in 1934. Note the distinctive tie. *(Addie Bassett Collection)*

Eddie Behean, manager, and the 1931 Casa del Desierto staff. *(Mojave River Valley Museum — Hazel Poe Hallock Collection)*

Barstow Harvey House manager Willy Riley and staff, 1930's. *(Rose Kuckivich Schmidt Collection)*

Barstow Harvey House, 1943. Irvin Krause, manager *(Mojave River Valley Museum — B. Stone Collection)*

In Barstow, the new Casa del Desierto became the fashionable spot to take a date on special occasions or to entertain out of town guests. Dynamic managers catered banquets and fraternal association dinners. At the onset of World War I, manager Loso did his best to serve the "Dough Boys" as endless troop and equipment trains jammed rails east and west. He received tremendous help from a strong local Red Cross groups of Barstow ladies who freely donated their time making and passing lunch baskets to the "boys". During World War II, USO volunteers performed similar services entirely on their own.

We know practically nothing about the earliest Harvey Girls, but while World War I heralded the beginning of our modern transportation system, it also roused the women's rights movement spurring females to leave their sheltered lives. During the 1920's and 30's eastern and midwestern ladies responded in droves to Santa Fe's ads calling for "young women of good character, attractive and intelligent, 18 to 30 . . ." They became the Harvey Girls so idyllically portrayed by the mid 40's MGM movie that one easily forgets their real counterparts. The signing of a Fred Harvey contract whereby the waitress pledged her bachelorhood for a year, shows how difficult it must have been for the system to keep their female help. This would apply as well for the need of matrons to watch over the girls' good character and see to their decorum. At Barstow, a continual influx of waitresses kept the customers satisfied and happy with the Harvey System.

For dining room service, early Harvey Girls wore a white full length pinafore with a stiff clerical collar accentuated by a tiny bow matching their dress, stockings and shoes; these were black for winter and white in summer. After World War I the uniform dress was softened by a white Elsie collar and contrasting bowtie. The dining room head waitress, "the wagon boss", sported a distinctive necktie instead of the regular bow. Although the later pinafore with a moderate decollectage was the standard apparel, aprons varied in fabrics and styles according to the formality of service at some Harvey Houses. The Barstow Girls fought early to discard their black dress for the cooler white one . . . they won in the mid 1930s.

Starting wages were only $17.50 a month including room and board plus tips. In 1919 the Barstow Harvey personnel joined Local No. 729 of the newly organized Hotel & Restaurant Alliance but, the long standing attitude of employers against any Unions immediately played havoc with their positions . . . they were soon replaced! While railroaders obtained substantial retirement benefits of their own, Fred Harvey personnel only received straight Social Security pensions almost a minimum rate, and that after it became mandatory.

Harvey Girls worked long hours, split shift fashion, attending two or three tables several times a day in the dining room plus their side work and lunch counter duties.

In most cases, the Harvey Girls joined the company to get away from a dull environment back home. Seeking freedom and independence, they escaped West secretly wishing for adventures and even dreaming of capturing a spouse. At the end of the trail, they found many suitors, mostly railroad men, and both parties set out to play the age old game of wooing and entertaining each other. On the local scene, equipped with good hiking shoes and armed with picnic baskets, the girls often banded together on desert expeditions riding in their date's old Model T. They visited mines and posed as prospectors for a portrait to send home meanwhile recording the trail's mishaps they had encountered. Close to the depot, they relaxed in their rooms or on the lawn, played tennis or croquet in the yard, attended dances and movies uptown, took a dip in local pools, rented bicycles for short rides, playfully pampered abandoned dogs, and even built snowmen during occasional storms. Yes, our Harvey Girls found time to enjoy themselves!

Many railroad towns boast their share of retired Harvey Girls, but at Barstow we proudly have a 40 year veteran waitress. She is Addie Park Bassett now the widow of another veteran of the system, the late Frank Bassett. On July 4, 1927, Addie followed and joined her sister, Jessie Park Potter, to work at the Vaughn Harvey House in New Mexico. Together they transferred to Barstow in 1928. Although Mrs. Bassett has served at

Harvey Girls attired for desert foot travel about 1920. Mary E. Willis, top right. *(Mojave River Valley Museum — copied from Desert Dispatch files)*

Early 1920's Barstow Harvey Girls taking a break. Top left is Nannie Burke, and standing in front is Nellie Warner (Howell). *(Garland Dittman Collection)*

Pauline & Vernon Carter (brother and sister) in 1922 at Murph's Plunge in North Barstow Addition. *(Mojave River Valley Museum — Carter Collection)*

John Sloan showing off his new Buick in the front of the Barstow Post Office Town. The two young ladies on the left may be Harvey Girls. *(Martha Burnau Col)*

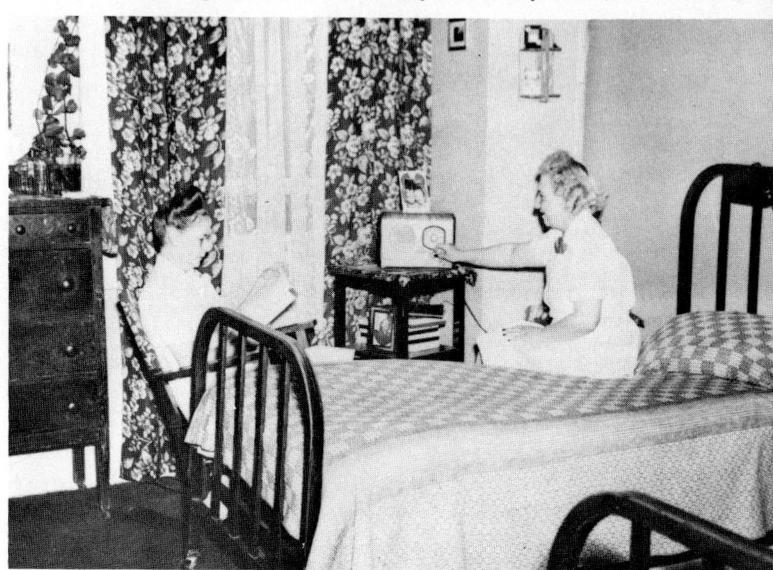

Comfortable and cozy. Effie V. Aleshire and Hazel B. Roberts (Noland-Wi veteran Harvey waitresses relaxing in their room at Barstow Harvey House *(Mojave River Valley Museum — B. Stone Collection, original Santa Fe Railway photo)*

Effie V. Aleshire, Troop Dog, and Addie P. Bassett. Troop Dog found a new hom Barstow Harvey House after being ousted from a troop train during WWII. *(Addie Collection, original Santa Fe Railway photo)*

Top: Harvey Girls on a 1928 expedition. Back row, L to R: Floyd Tucker, Olive Durbin, Ruby Douglas. Front: Addie Park (Bassett), Myrtle Stiles, and Jessie Park Potter. *(Addie Bassett Collection)*

Bottom: Late 1920's Santa Fe employees: Joe Park & Earl Potter, conductors: Charles Park, engineer: (front) Orville Park, railroad clerk. (Note desert cooler on stilts at top left.) *(Addie Bassett Collection)*

other Houses, most of her career was spent here. She recalls and provides a pictorial record of the many changes that occurred in the System over the years — from the time a "gong" attendant inspected prospective patrons for dress requirements to the time paper cups replaced the fine glassware. She tells of managers keeping extra dark alpaca jackets to rescue unaware customers caught without coat and tie but desiring service in the dining room. She didn't forget the pains in her arms and shoulders nor the interminable hours spent slicing mountains of bread and serving hungry battle bound GI's as well as the returning war prisoners. She remembers the shut down of the hotel and near closure of the dining room after the depression . . .

In the mid 1930's passengers opted for meals on board trains or turned to airplanes and automobiles for travel starting the long death rattle of Fred Harvey rail passenger services and his association with Santa Fe.

These two Pacific Coast Borax 20 Mule Team wagons stood many years in the park east of the Casa del Desierto. Photo taken in the 1930's after a severe snow storm, an unusual desert event. *(Addie Bassett Collection)*

Westbound Hi-Level El Capitan stopped in the front of Barstow depot and Harvey House. Note the Railway Express east on the bottom right of the photo. (*Courtesy of Santa Fe Railway, photo by Don Erb.*)

Only the short revival and bustle during World War II (1942-47) postponed the ultimate end. On "June 5, 1959, Mrs. Evelyn F. Pattison leased from Santa Fe a portion of the Station to be used as site for Restaurant and Newsstand facilities". This was the forepart of the Case del Desierto which was operated mostly for the convenience of railroad employees almost another twelve years before it closed down with the advent of Amtrak.

After the restaurant closure, rumors began to spread of an impending destruction of the entire property, although Santa Fe used the premises for work shops until February 2, 1976, upon the completion of the new class-

Unidentified Barstow Harvey Girls and companion posing for a portrait to send home. *(Agnes Copp Collection)*

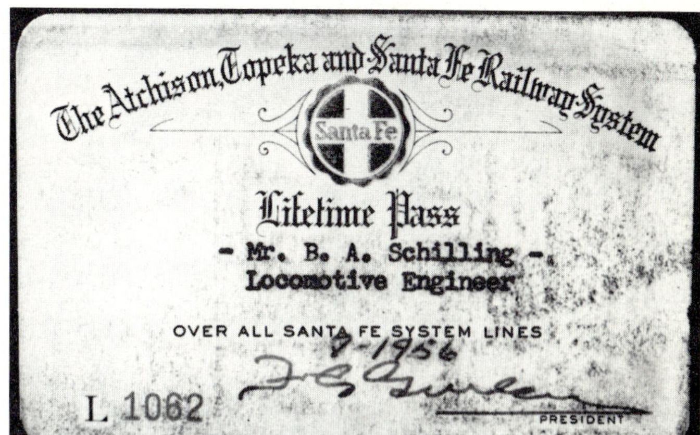

Mojave River Valley Museum *(B.A. Schilling Collection)*

Two Barstow Harvey Girls, Addie Park Bassett and Jessie Park Potter, and cook, Frank Bassett, posing on the veranda between the main building and the girl's dormitory (left). *(Addie Bassett Collection)*

Patrons waiting for the Harvey House manager to open the restaurant doors. The attendant (in foreground) facing the patrons banged a coded message on his gong to the staff inside. *(Mojave River Valley Museum — Hazel Poe Hallock Collection)*

A mid 1910's view of Santa Fe passenger yard and repair facilities. Dillingham General Merchandise Store (east side) and lumber yard on the right. Car repair shed mid photo. *(Martha Burnau Collection)*

Engine 2206 crew and others behind the Barstow Harvey House laundry in 1905: L to R: a boomer switchman; — Walker; V.H. Tibbetts & George Davidson, helpers; G.W. Lupton, trainmaster, David B. Absalon, engine herder. Engineer Rockwell. Engineer Richardson, and Charles H. McCormick, general yard master, unknown fireman in cab window. *(Santa Fe Magazine clipping — McCoy Collection)*

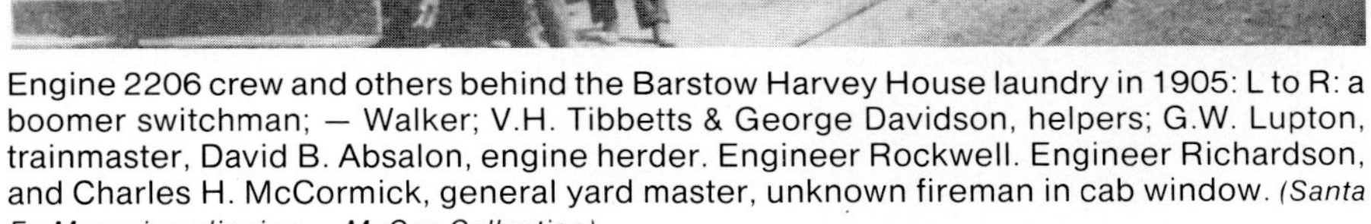

Late 1920's aerial view of the Santa Fe round house drawing the storehouse, mechanic shed and power house. The site of the old roundhouse was east (bottom right) of the power house. *(Clarence Crooks Collection)*

ification yards on the west of B Hill. Beginning in 1974, concerned groups of citizens formed committees and worked to "Save the Harvey House". Countless hours and energy were, and are still being, spent toward the acquisition of the property, to find ways to renovate and give it a new life. The Mojave River Valley Museum devoted their 1975 BBQ program in honor of the local former Harvey Girls. Their participation brought back flavors of a past romantic age. News media, local as well as far away, drummed public interest stories while Santa Fe razed parts of the grand old complex. Conservation appeals were heard and the Railroad proved their good faith by postponing a complete removal of the buildings and by appointing the City of Barstow their agent. The "Save the Harvey House" organizations are prevented from realizing their dreams by a dilemma: they can not obtain proper funding because they do not have proprietary rights nor a tenant lease from Santa Fe, and, on the other hand, they can not get the lease because they lack the necessary monies required for a project of this magnitude. On the positive side, registration at both the federal and state levels, was secured and the Casa del Desierto is on the National Register of Historic Places No. 4375, and on the California Register of Historic Landmarks No. 892. It seems that such official recognition should guarantee the perpetuity of the building . . . apparently it does not.

The fate of the Harvey House will be decided on April 8, 1980, when Barstow voters choose whether or not the City of Barstow should accept the responsibility of saving the structure. The restoration and re-use would boost the City re-development projects scheduled for that area giving the town a visual and tangible example of their proud historic heritage. Yes, as long as the Casa del Desierto remains there is still hope for a renewed life.

Santa Fe Railway's Barstow, California facilities are lighted for night operations. Center, background, is the passenger station, with the Hi-Level El Capitan ready to continue its westbound run to Los Angeles. Late 1950's, early 60's. *(Courtesy of Santa Fe Railway, photo by Don Erb)*

Aerial view, Feb. 2, 1976 of Santa Fe's old railyards and other facilities. *(Courtesy of Santa Fe Railway — Zeitelhack Collection)*

BIBLIOGRAPHICAL NOTES

The amount of references used for this project was tremendous. Many books, newspapers, and magazine articles were read. Much was learned studying magnifications of photographs and consulting the San Bernardino County's archival withholdings. We shall list here only the major source references.

BOOKS:

Bryant, Keith L., Jr. "History of the Atchison, Topeka & Santa Fe Railway",
Macmillan Publishing Co., N.Y. 1974.

Henderson, James David, "Meals by Fred Harvey", Texas Christian University, 1969.

Keeling, Patricia Jernigan, Editor, "Once Upon A Desert", Mojave River Valley
Museum Assn., Barstow, Ca. 1976.

Marshall, James, "Santa Fe, the Railroad that Built an Empire",
Random House, N.Y., 1945

Myrick, David F., "Railroads of Nevada and Eastern California" Vol. II,
Howell-North Books, Berkeley, Ca. 1963.

DOCUMENTS ON MICROFILM:

Bureau of Land Management, Riverside Office, Tract Books, Sacramento, Ca. Roll #12.

National Archives of the United States, Washington, D.C.:
San Bernardino County 1900 Census, CA-T623-97.
Record of Appointments of Postmasters, CA-841-12.

San Bernardino County Archives:
Board of Supervisors Minute Books.
Court House, Trial briefs.
Recorder's Office:
Agreement books,
Contract books,
Deed books,
Lease books,
Map books,
Mining District and Misc. books,
Miscellaneous books.
Road Department: Map files.

INTERVIEWS & PERSONAL CORRESPONDENCE:

Addie Park Bassett.
Mr. & Mrs. Ray L. Conaway.
Clarence B. Crooks.
Rex Dillingham.
Mr. & Mrs. Fred Gibson.
Patricia Jernigan Keeling.
Mr. & Mrs. Gale Kenyon.
Mr. & Mrs. Orville Lewis.
Mrs. Richard H. Miers.
Myrum James Mudgett.
Mr. & Mrs. Joseph B. Mulcahy.
Mr. & Mrs. Donald I. Pattison.
Willis Pinkerton.
Southern Pacific Land Company.

MISCELLANY:

Barstow Harvey House Society material; David Ottalini tape-program,
Mojave River Valley Museum Assn. Library.

NEWSPAPERS:

Barstow Printer, Barstow, Ca., back files at the Desert Dispatch Office.
Calico Print, Calico & Daggett, Ca. Bancroft Library micro. FfF 850- C 15.
Daily Courier, San Bernardino, Ca., Jan. 21 thru Dec. 31, 1892; Bancroft Library NMP 242.
Weekly Courier, San Bernardino, Ca., Mar. 2 thru Aug. 26, 1893; Bancroft Library NMP 266.
Desert Dispatch, Barstow, Ca., feature stories, news items and Garland Dittman series.
The Needles Eye, Needles, Ca., June 14, 1891 thru Dec 27, 1894; Bell & Howell micro.
Newspaper Miscellany (San Diegan); Bancroft Library, NMP 4290.
Sun-Telegram, San Bernardino, Ca., news clippings and feature stories.
Weekly Times, San Bernardino, Ca., Mar 20, 1880 thru Dec 24, 1887; Bancroft Library NMP 269.

PERIODICALS:

Santa Fe Magazine, Santa Fe Railway, Chicago, Il., undated & dated clippings,
    also Dec. 1943 issue.
Western States Jewish Historical Quarterly, Southern California Jewish Historical Society,
    Santa Monica, Ca., Norton B. Stern, O.D., Editor; back issues
    Herb Stein Collection.

PHOTOGRAPHS:

Mojave River Valley Museum Collection.
Patricia Jernigan Keeling Collection.

California Southern Railroad

All Rail Line between
National City, San Diego and Los Angeles,
And Points East and West.

Close Connections made at Barstow with A. & P. R. R. and at Los Angeles with S. P. R. R. Through tickets to eastern points, with choice of routes.

Pullman Sleeping Cars on Passenger Trains.

Time Table taking effect Apr. 4, 1885.

daily	daily.		daily	daily
2 00 P M	7 00 A M	..Los Angeles.	9 10 P M	12 20 P M
2 23	7 21	..San Gabriel..	8 50	11 56 A M
3 18	8 20	....Pomona...	7 55	10 56
4 15	9 15 A M	AR Colton LV.	6 55 P M	10 00
daily	ex sud'y		ex sud'y	daily
7 45	9 30 A M	LV Colton AR.	5 35 P M	7 50 A M
8 00	9 44	....Citrus....	5 21	7 8
9 30	10 49	....Perris.....	4 10	6 15
12 15 A M	1 56 P M	..Fall Brook...	1 03	3 45
2 45	3 15	..Oceanside...	11 25 P M	2 15 A M
6 30	6 05	AR San Diego LV	8 05	10 45 P M
7 00 A M	6 35 P M	.National City.	7 30 A M	10 00 P M
ex sud'y	ex sud'y		ex sud'y	ex sud'y
5 30 P M	10 15 A M	LV Citrus AR	5 15 P M	8 45 A M
5 45	10 30	Ar Riv'rside LV	5 00	8 30

	daily		daily
	9 20 A M	....Colton......	6 25 P M
	9 40	San Bernardino	6 05
	12 10 PM	.....Victor.....	4 03
	1 30	..Barstow..	2 55

Trains are run on Pacific Standard time.

Passengers will save from ten (10) to one dollar and ten cents (1.10) by purchasing their tickets of the Agent before entering the cars.

Tickets can be purchased at the General Ticket office, San Diego, during the day, and sleeper taken at the foot of E street after 8 p. m.

For rates of freight or fare, address California Southern Railroad Agents, or.

J. N. VICTOR,
Superintendent.
Colton,
Cal.

H. B. WILKINS,
Gen. Frt. & Pass' Agent.
San Diego, Cal.

The time table above contains a misprint: April 4, 1885 (sic). The California Southern Junction with the main A & P line was effected on November 15, 1885. At the time the junction was called Waterman and renamed Barstow only in January, 1886, by the railroad company. *(The San Diegan, San Diego, CA. May 11, 1886 — p.6, c. 2.)*